WATERLOO

Script: TemPoe
Artwork: Mor
Colours: Florent Daniel
Historical supervision: Patrice Courcelle

We would like to thank Patrice Courcelle, Etienne Claude, Laurence Nelis, Marie-Isabelle Legrand, the "ASBL Bataille de Waterloo 1815", the reenactment teams, and more particularly Arnaud Olbrechts, Franky Simon and Franck Samson, Tanguy de Ghellinck, as well as Josette Champt and the "Maison du Tourisme des Ardennes Brabançonnes" for their participation in this historic reconstruction in graphic novel form.

www.facebook.com/sandawe
© Sandawe, 2015.
www.sandawe.com, contact@sandawe.com

Copyright : April 2015; D/2015/12.351/10
ISBN 978-2-930623-50-4

First Edition

Translation and lettering: BOOM!, Wingene

All translation and reproduction rights reserved in all countries. It is strictly forbidden, except with written prior agreement from the publisher, to partially or completely reproduce this work, by whatever process (including photocopying or digitalization), to store it in a data bank or to provide it to the public. Copying or reproduction constitutes an infringement punishable by law provided by the law of March 11 1957 on the protection of authors' rights.

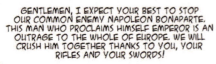

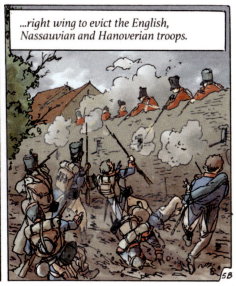

The Drouet d'Erlon battalions are lined up from the Belle Alliance crossroads to Papelotte Farm. With Ney leading them, they advance straight ahead towards the Anglo-Dutch line. The Haie-Sainte is at the end on their left.

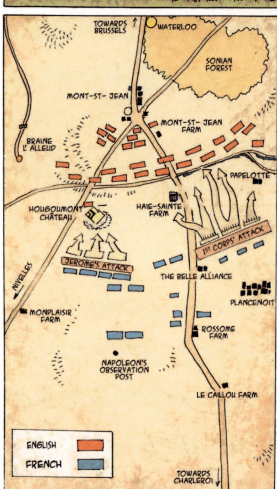

The Prince of Orange.

THE BATTLE IS JOINED, GENERAL!

THE FRENCH ARE LAUNCHING A FRONTAL ATTACK ON OUR TROOPS!

LET US HOPE OUR BRIGADES CONTAIN THE ONSLAUGHT!

LOOK! THEY HAVE ALREADY REACHED THE HANOVERIANS AT THE HAIE-SAINTE!

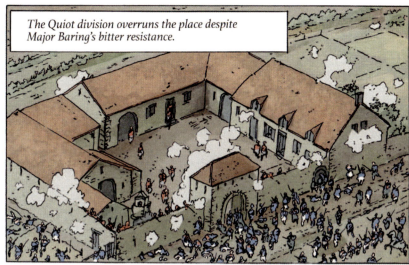
The Quiot division overruns the place despite Major Baring's bitter resistance.

IMMEDIATELY SEND KIELMANSEGG'S BATTALION TO REINFORCE BARING AND TELL PICTON TO STAY READY!

The order is immediately executed.

But the Hanoverian soldiers cannot resist the cuirassiers' brutal assault.

FALL BACK!

As to General Picton...

I SAY, THESE FRENCH ARE BEING PERSISTENT! BUT TAKE MY WORD, THEY WILL NOT PASS!

Meanwhile the French divisions of Donzelot and Marcognet keep advancing.

FOR THE EMPEROR!

WE HAVE REACHED THE OHAIN PATH!

But on the ridge's other side...

ON MY MARK!

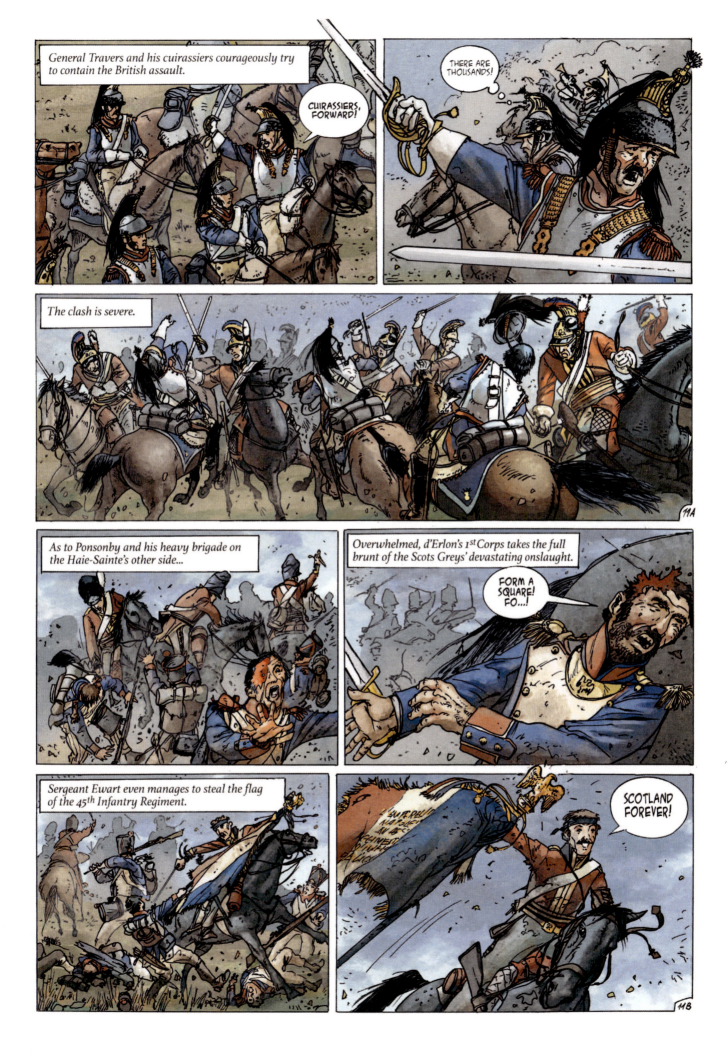

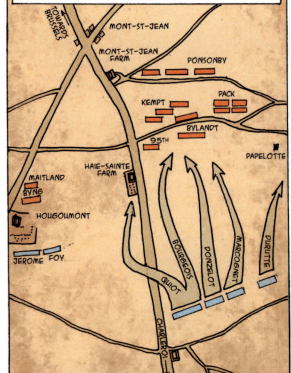

It is almost 3pm. The exhausted combatants fall back to regain their strength. The French attack broke on the allied front and Drouet d'Erlon's divisions failed to take the Haie-Sainte and Papelotte Farms. The French versus the Allies: everyone remains in place.

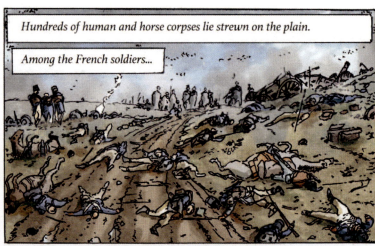

Hundreds of human and horse corpses lie strewn on the plain.

Among the French soldiers...

...as well as the allied forces.

Le Caillou Farm...

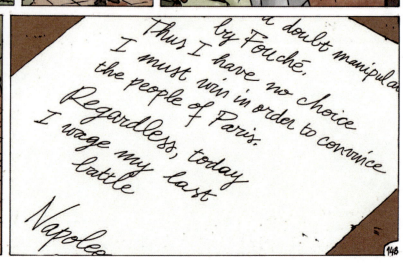

...no doubt manipulated by Fouché, thus I have no choice. I must win in order to convince the people of Paris. Regardless, today I wage my last battle.

Napoleon

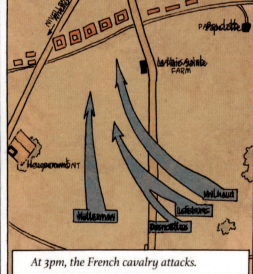

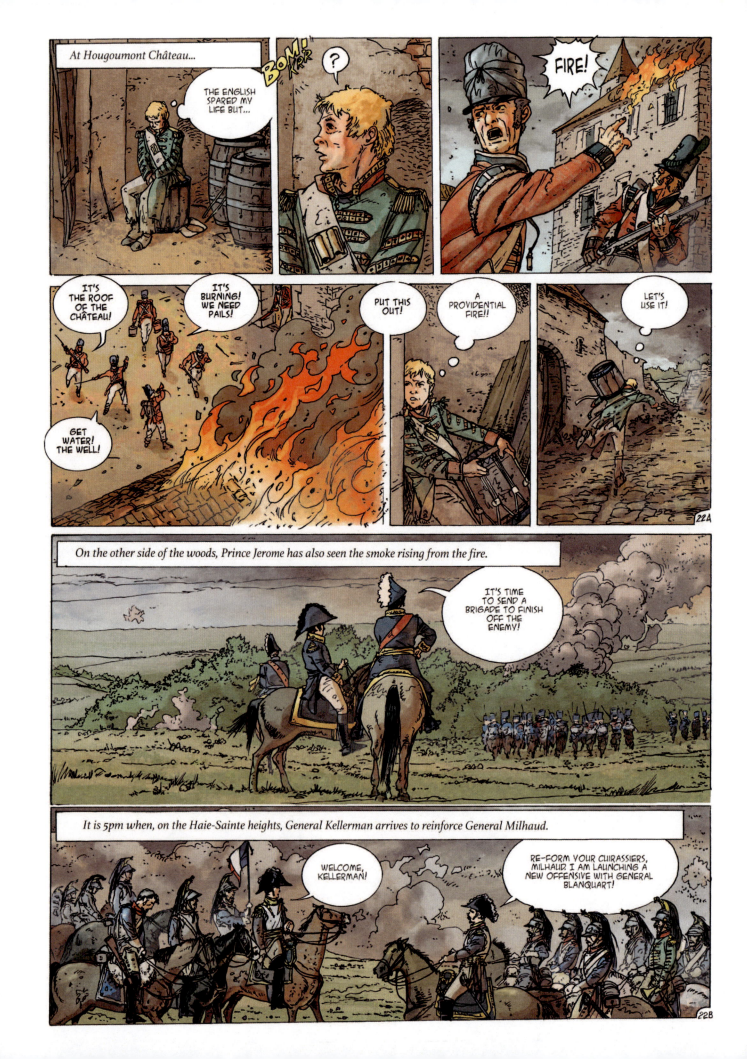

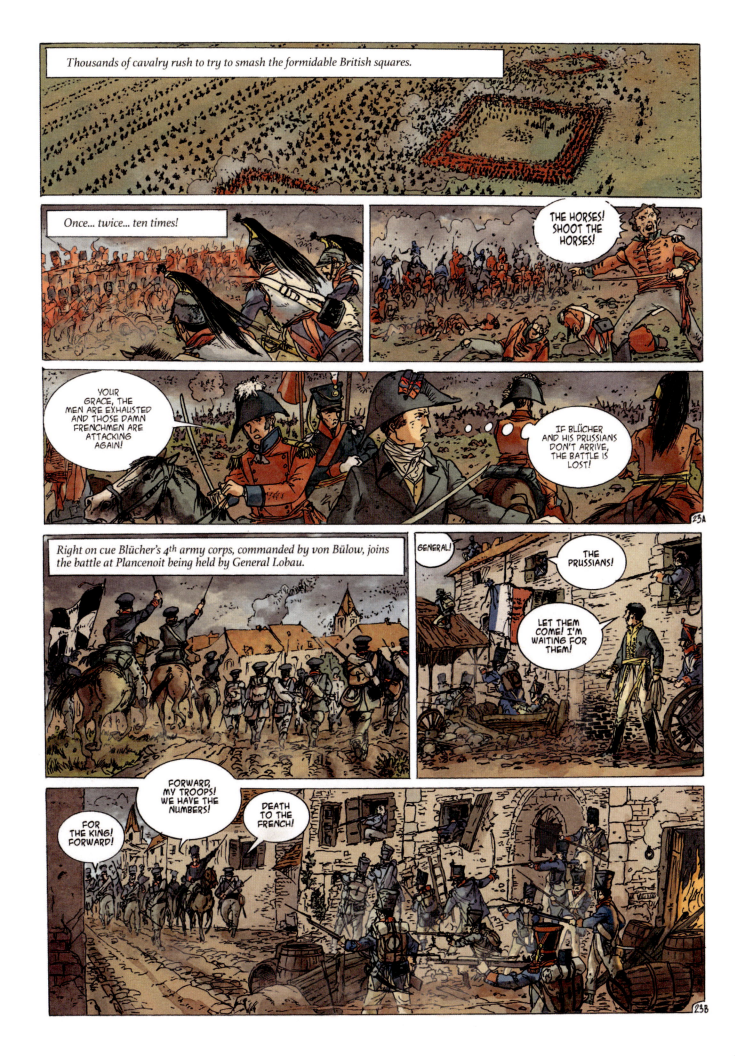

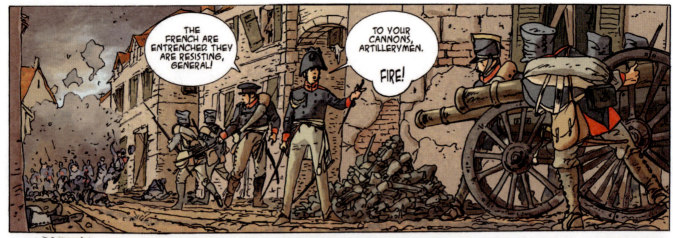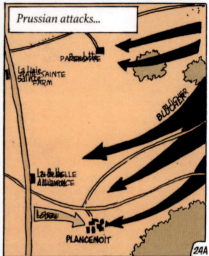

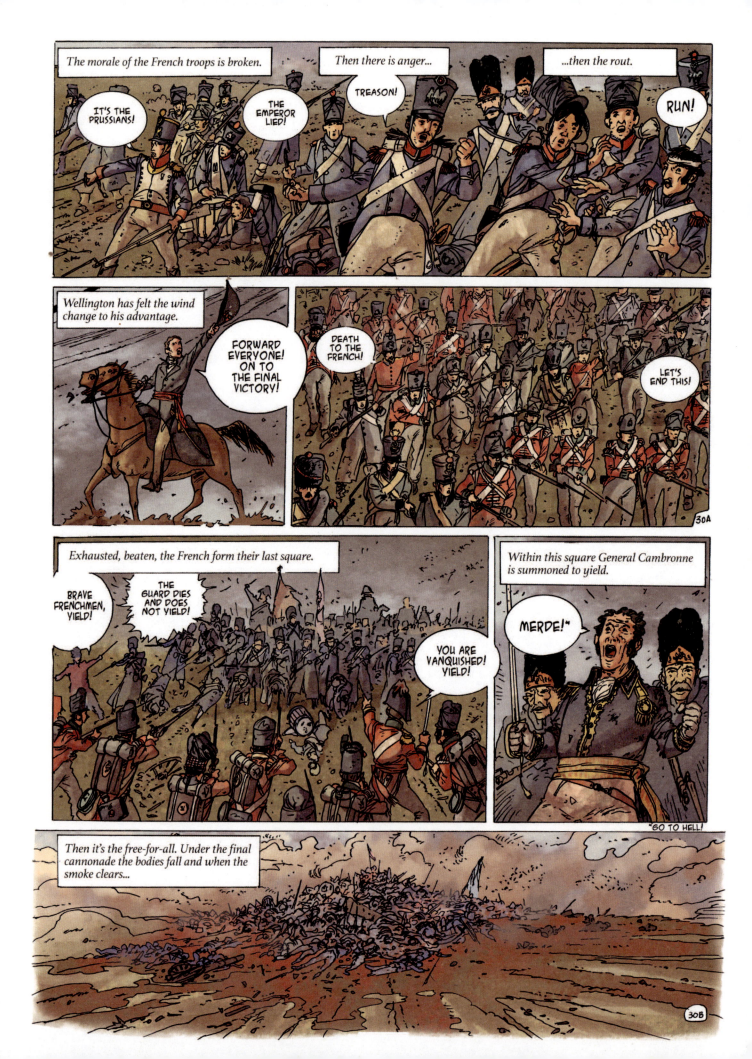

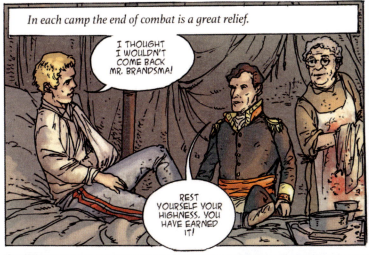

MAYBE THIS TUESDAY
Graphic novel

Achilles, a man in his forties, has just buried his parents. He likes to sit on the beach below his house and watch the passing ships heading for the high seas. So much so that one evening he falls asleep sitting on his chair with both feet firmly buried in the sand. However, when he awakes he is unable to move: during the night he has literally taken root. As a huge storm brews over his island, a seagull flies towards him.
The seagull, which can talk, informs Achilles on which day of the week he will die: a Tuesday. But which one? That's the question.
Fortunately today is a Wednesday. The tide is rising and will soon flood the beach. If the seagull is telling the truth Achilles needs to uproot himself quickly to avoid drowning. It would appear that the time has come for him to cease contemplating passing ships...

http://www.amazon.fr/Maybe-this-Tuesday-Nicolas-Vadot/dp/2930623071